Writer's Guide
2025 EDITION

MASTERING AMAZON PUBLISHING:

A COMPREHENSIVE GUIDE TO SUCCESS FOR INDIE AUTHORS

Multi-Award-Winning-Author
B Alan Bourgeois

Mastering Amazon Publishing

B Alan Bourgeois

Mastering Amazon Publishing: A Comprehensive Guide to Success for Indie Authors

© B Alan Bourgeois 2025

All rights reserved. No part of this publication may be reproduced, stored in a retrieval system, or transmitted in any form or by any means, electronic, mechanical, photocopying, recording, or otherwise, without the prior written permission of the publisher.

The information and opinions expressed in this book are believed to be accurate and reliable, but no responsibility or liability is assumed by the publisher for any errors, omissions, or any damages caused by the use of these products, procedures, or methods presented herein.

The book is sold and distributed on an "as is" basis without warranties of any kind, either expressed or implied, including but not limited to warranties of merchantability or fitness for a particular purpose. The purchaser or reader of this book assumes complete responsibility for the use of these materials and information.

Any legal disputes arising from the use of this book shall be governed by the laws of the jurisdiction where the book was purchased, without regard to its conflict of law provisions, and shall be resolved exclusively in the courts of that jurisdiction.

ISBN: 979-8-3483-9943-6

Publisher: Bourgeois Media & Consulting (BourgeoisMedia.com)

Mastering Amazon Publishing

B ALAN BOUERGEOIS

STORYTELLING LITERACY & HERITAGE

Thank you for purchasing this limited edition book, offered in celebration of the author's 50-year milestone. Proceeds from your purchase support the Texas Authors Institute of History, a museum founded by the author in 2015, dedicated to preserving the legacy of Texas authors.

https://TexasAuthors.Institute

B Alan Bourgeois

Dear Fellow Authors,

I'm delighted to introduce this book—and every guide in this series—as a short, easy-to-read resource designed to help you succeed in your writing journey. As writers, our true passion lies in creating stories, and I understand that delving into the business side of publishing might not be where we wish to spend most of our time.

That's why I've made a conscious effort to keep things simple and straightforward, focusing on practical advice without unnecessary fluff. You'll find that some concepts overlap between books, and that's intentional—to reinforce key ideas and ensure that whichever guide you pick up, you're equipped with valuable tools to enhance your success.

I genuinely hope you find these guides enjoyable and helpful. Your feedback means the world to me, and I look forward to hearing about your experiences and triumphs.

Happy writing, and here's to your continued success!

Mastering Amazon Publishing

Introduction

Welcome to "Mastering Amazon Publishing: A Comprehensive Guide to Success for Indie Authors"

In today's digital age, the opportunities for indie authors to publish and distribute their work have never been greater. Among the many platforms available, Amazon stands out as a powerful and accessible tool for self-publishing. However, navigating its complex ecosystem can be daunting, even for seasoned authors. This is where "Mastering Amazon Publishing" comes in.

Whether you're a first-time author or an experienced writer looking to maximize your success, this comprehensive guide is designed to help you understand and leverage the full potential of Amazon's publishing platform. From setting up your KDP account to optimizing your book's visibility, this book covers every aspect of the publishing journey.

Why Amazon?

Amazon's Kindle Direct Publishing (KDP) platform revolutionized the way authors bring their stories to readers. With millions of potential readers worldwide, Amazon offers unmatched reach and exposure. But with great power comes great complexity. Understanding the intricacies of Amazon's policies, algorithms, and tools is crucial to standing out in a crowded market.

What You Will Learn

"Mastering Amazon Publishing" is divided into two main parts: **Beyond the Amazon Bubble** and **Amazon Advantage**. Each section is designed to equip you with the knowledge and strategies needed to thrive in the world of self-publishing.

Part One: Beyond the Amazon Bubble

In this section, we delve into the potential pitfalls of relying solely on Amazon for your publishing needs. You'll learn about:

- The limitations of exclusive distribution and how to expand your reach.
- The inner workings of Amazon's ecosystem and how to optimize your presence.
- Evaluating the pros and cons of Amazon's various programs and services.
- Strategies for maximizing royalties and navigating the shifting sands of Amazon's policies.
- The importance of a multi-platform approach to reach a diverse readership.

Part Two: Amazon Advantage

Here, we focus on harnessing the unique advantages that Amazon offers. You'll discover:

- How to leverage Amazon's global reach and self-publishing ease.
- The benefits of retaining creative and financial control with KDP.

Mastering Amazon Publishing

- Advanced strategies for maximizing profits through competitive eBook royalties.
- Quick and effective methods for publishing both eBooks and paperbacks.
- Techniques for amplifying your reach with Amazon Advertising and Kindle Unlimited.
- The power of Print-On-Demand services and managing customer reviews.
- Optimizing your author profile with Amazon Author Central for enhanced visibility.

Real-Life Success Stories

Throughout this guide, you'll find real-life case studies of indie authors who have successfully navigated Amazon's platform. These stories provide practical insights and inspiration, demonstrating how the strategies outlined in this book can lead to tangible success.

Your Journey to Success

"Mastering Amazon Publishing" is more than just a guide; it's your roadmap to success in the self-publishing world. By the end of this book, you will have a deep understanding of how to navigate Amazon's platform, make informed decisions, and implement effective strategies to reach your publishing goals.

Embark on this journey with us, and let's unlock the full potential of your writing career together.

Welcome to your guide to mastering Amazon publishing. Let's get started!

Chapters

Section 1
Beyond the Amazon Bubble: Expanding Your Reach as an Author

1. The Pitfalls of Limited Distribution — 12
2. Navigating the Amazon Jungle — 19
3. Weighing the Pros and Cons — 25
4. Royalties in the eBook World — 29
5. Navigating the Shifting Sands — 33
6. The Amazon Conundrum — 36
7. Navigating Amazon's Review Policies — 40
8. Navigating Algorithm Dependency on Amazon — 44
9. Weighing the Pros and Cons of Amazon's KDP Select Exclusivity Period — 48
10. Navigating the Waters of eBook Pricing — 52

Mastering Amazon Publishing

Section 2
Amazon Advantage
Your Path to Publishing Success

1. The Global Reach of Amazon	58
2. The Ease of Self-Publishing with Amazon's	
3. KDP Platform	62
4. Empowering Authors Retaining Control with Amazon KDP	66
5. Maximizing Profits Amazon's Competitive eBook	
6. Royalties For Authors	70
7. Rapid Results: Quick eBook and Paperback	
8. Publishing with Amazon KDP	74
9. Amplify Your Reach: Amazon Advertising for Authors	79
10. Unleash Your Earnings: Kindle Unlimited for Authors	83
11. The Power of Print-On-Demand	87
12. Harnessing the Power of Customer Reviews	91
13. Amazon Author Central	95
About the Author	99
Other Books by the Author in this Series	100

Section 1
Beyond the Amazon Bubble: Expanding Your Reach as an Author

1
The Pitfalls of Limited Distribution

Why Exclusively Publishing on Amazon May Limit Your Reach

Amazon, with its vast reach and customer base, has become a go-to platform for many authors looking to self-publish their books. While Amazon is undeniably a powerful player in the book-selling industry, there's a growing concern about the potential downsides of exclusively publishing on this platform. One significant drawback is limited distribution. In this chapter, we'll delve into why relying solely on Amazon might cause you to miss out on potential readers from other platforms and bookstores.

The Dominance of Amazon

Amazon's dominance in the online retail world is unparalleled. It boasts millions of customers and an extensive network of distribution centers worldwide. For authors, this means easy access to a global audience and a user-friendly platform for publishing and marketing books.

However, while Amazon's reach is impressive, it's essential to remember that it's not the only player in the book-selling game. Several other platforms and traditional bookstores cater to a diverse readership. Ignoring these alternatives can be a missed opportunity.

The Pitfalls of Exclusivity

Amazon offers a program called KDP Select, which encourages authors to publish exclusively on Amazon for 90-day periods. While this program has its benefits, including promotional tools and Kindle Unlimited participation, it comes with a significant trade-off: limited distribution.

Here are some key reasons why exclusively publishing on Amazon may limit your reach:

Missing Out on Other eBook Retailers: By committing to Amazon exclusively, you're forfeiting the chance to sell your eBook through other popular platforms like Apple Books, Barnes & Noble Nook, Kobo, and Google Play Books. These platforms have their user bases, and you're excluding potential readers who prefer these alternatives.

For example, an author who published exclusively on Amazon noticed a plateau in sales after a few months. They decided to expand their distribution to include Apple Books and Kobo, resulting in a 30% increase in overall sales and a significant boost in reader engagement from users who favored those platforms.

Excluding Print Book Lovers: Amazon dominates the eBook market, but it's just one piece of the publishing puzzle. Readers who prefer physical books often visit traditional bookstores, and they may not have access to your book if it's exclusive to Amazon.

Consider the case of an author whose eBook was successful on Amazon, but they found that many potential readers were requesting a print version. By using a print-on-demand service

Mastering Amazon Publishing

that distributes to local bookstores, they were able to meet the demand and significantly increase their sales.

Reduced Visibility in Physical Stores: If you dream of seeing your book on the shelves of local bookstores, exclusively publishing on Amazon won't help. Physical retailers typically prefer to work with distributors that offer a wide range of titles, not just Amazon-exclusive ones.

An author who published a memoir found that their local bookstore was eager to stock their book, but only if it was available through traditional distribution channels. By using services like IngramSpark, the author managed to get their book into multiple stores, enhancing their visibility and credibility within the community.

Limited Global Reach: While Amazon is available in numerous countries, local eBook retailers often have a more significant presence in specific regions. Publishing exclusively on Amazon may hinder your ability to reach readers in these areas.

For instance, a travel guide author expanded their distribution to include local eBook retailers in Europe and Asia, resulting in a substantial increase in sales from those regions. This move helped them build a global readership that would have been missed by relying solely on Amazon.

Diverse Readership: Different platforms attract different types of readers. By limiting your book's availability to one platform, you miss the chance to cater to a diverse audience of readers with varying preferences.

A fantasy author found that while Amazon's algorithm helped them reach a wide audience initially, expanding to platforms like

Kobo and Google Play Books allowed them to tap into niche markets that were highly engaged and passionate about their genre.

The Importance of a Multi-Platform Approach

To maximize your book's potential reach, consider a multi-platform approach. This means making your book available on Amazon and other eBook retailers, both in digital and print formats. Here are some advantages of this approach:

Expanded Reach: Your book becomes accessible to a broader audience, including readers who prefer specific eBook platforms or formats.

Increased Visibility: Being on multiple platforms can improve your book's visibility and discoverability.

For example, an author who initially launched their book exclusively on Amazon saw a 40% increase in visibility and sales after expanding to multiple platforms, including Apple Books and Barnes & Noble Nook. This approach helped them reach a wider audience and gain more traction in the competitive market.

Print Book Options: Readers who prefer physical copies can purchase your book from their local bookstores or online retailers.

A romance author used print-on-demand services like IngramSpark to make their book available in physical form. This allowed them to cater to readers who prefer printed books, resulting in higher overall sales and more satisfied customers.

Mastering Amazon Publishing

Global Accessibility: Reach readers in different regions by leveraging local eBook retailers with a strong regional presence.

An author of a historical fiction novel found that by distributing their book through local retailers in Europe, they were able to connect with readers who might not have discovered their work through Amazon alone. This strategy helped them build a loyal international readership.

Diverse Audience: Cater to a wider variety of readers with different preferences and habits.

A science fiction author saw their readership diversify after making their book available on multiple platforms. Different platforms attracted readers with specific interests, helping the author build a more robust and engaged fan base.

Case Study: The Multi-Platform Success of "The Indie Author Advantage"

Consider the example of "The Indie Author Advantage," a book that was initially published exclusively on Amazon. While the book saw moderate success, the author decided to expand its distribution to other platforms, including Apple Books, Kobo, and local bookstores. This move resulted in a significant increase in sales and readership. By making the book available in multiple formats and on various platforms, the author was able to reach a more diverse and global audience.

Practical Steps for Expanding Distribution

1. **Research Alternative Platforms:** Investigate other eBook retailers and distributors like Apple Books, Barnes & Noble Nook, Kobo, and Google Play Books. Each

platform has its own submission process and requirements.
2. **Format Your Book for Multiple Platforms:** Ensure your book is formatted correctly for each platform. This might involve creating different versions of your eBook to meet the specific requirements of each retailer.
3. **Use Aggregators:** Consider using aggregators like Smashwords or Draft2Digital, which can distribute your book to multiple retailers simultaneously. These services simplify the process of reaching a wider audience.
4. **Print on Demand (POD):** Utilize print-on-demand services like IngramSpark or Blurb to make your book available in physical form. This allows readers who prefer print copies to access your book without the need for large print runs.
5. **Local Bookstores and Libraries:** Reach out to local bookstores and libraries to see if they would be interested in carrying your book. Many independent bookstores are open to stocking books from local authors.
6. **Marketing Across Platforms:** Develop a marketing strategy that promotes your book across all the platforms it's available on. Use social media, email newsletters, and author websites to inform readers about where they can find your book.

Balancing Exclusivity and Wider Distribution

While it's important to diversify your distribution channels, there are scenarios where exclusivity with Amazon's KDP Select might be beneficial, particularly for new authors looking to leverage Amazon's promotional tools. However, as your author brand grows, expanding to other platforms can help sustain long-term success and reach a more varied readership.

Mastering Amazon Publishing

While Amazon offers tremendous opportunities for self-published authors, exclusive publishing on this platform may limit your book's distribution. To reach a wider audience and diversify your readership, consider making your book available on multiple platforms and in various formats. By doing so, you can increase your book's chances of success and connect with readers who prefer alternative avenues for discovering and enjoying great literature. Balancing exclusivity with a broader distribution strategy can help you maximize your book's potential and achieve lasting success in the competitive world of publishing.

2
Navigating the Amazon Jungle

Understanding Amazon's Ecosystem

Amazon is more than just an online retailer; it's a complex ecosystem that encompasses eBooks, print-on-demand services, audiobook creation, and a variety of marketing and promotional tools. For an author, understanding how to navigate this jungle is crucial for maximizing your book's potential.

Amazon offers several key services to authors:

- **Kindle Direct Publishing (KDP)**: For eBooks and print-on-demand paperbacks.
- **Kindle Unlimited (KU)**: A subscription service that allows readers to access a vast library of eBooks.
- **Amazon Advertising**: A platform to create and manage ads for your books.
- **Amazon Author Central**: A hub where authors can manage their author profiles and track their book sales.

Optimizing Your Book Listing

To make the most out of Amazon, it's vital to optimize your book listing. This involves several components:

Mastering Amazon Publishing

Title and Subtitle: Make sure your title is compelling and includes keywords that potential readers might search for. Your subtitle should provide additional context or highlight a key benefit of your book.

Book Description: Your book description should be engaging and persuasive. It needs to grab the reader's attention, provide a brief summary of what the book is about, and highlight what makes your book unique. Use HTML formatting to make the description more readable and visually appealing.

Keywords: Amazon allows you to enter keywords that help your book appear in search results. Research and choose keywords that are relevant and have a good search volume.

Categories: Selecting the right categories is crucial for visibility. Amazon allows you to choose up to two categories, but you can request additional ones by contacting Amazon support. Aim for categories that are relevant but not overly competitive.

Author Page: Utilize Amazon Author Central to create a detailed author page. Include a professional author photo, a biography, links to your social media profiles, and any other relevant information. This helps build your author brand and connect with readers.

Leveraging Kindle Unlimited

Kindle Unlimited (KU) can be a double-edged sword. While it offers an opportunity to reach a large audience of avid readers, it also requires exclusivity, meaning your eBook cannot be available on other platforms while enrolled in KU.

Advantages:

- Increased Visibility: Books in KU often receive higher visibility on Amazon, including more prominent placement in search results and recommendations.
- Page Reads Revenue: You earn money based on the number of pages read by KU subscribers, providing an additional revenue stream.

Disadvantages:

- Exclusivity Requirement: Your eBook cannot be available on other platforms while enrolled in KU, limiting your distribution.
- Payment Variability: The amount you earn per page read can vary month to month, making income less predictable.

Utilizing Amazon Advertising

Amazon Advertising is a powerful tool for increasing your book's visibility and driving sales. There are several types of ads you can use:

Sponsored Products: These ads appear within search results and on product detail pages. They are highly effective for targeting specific keywords.

Sponsored Brands: These ads appear at the top of search results and include your book's cover, a custom headline, and a logo. They are great for building brand awareness.

Lockscreen Ads: These ads appear on the lock screens of Kindle devices. They are useful for targeting avid Kindle readers.

Mastering Amazon Publishing

To create successful ad campaigns:

- **Research Keywords**: Use tools like Amazon's Keyword Planner to find relevant keywords with good search volume.
- **Monitor and Adjust**: Regularly check your ad performance and make adjustments as needed to optimize your ROI.
- **Test Different Ad Types**: Experiment with different ad formats to see which ones work best for your book.

Navigating Amazon's Review Policies

Reviews are critical for the success of your book on Amazon. However, Amazon has strict policies to prevent manipulation and ensure the authenticity of reviews.

Do's:

- **Encourage Genuine Reviews**: Ask readers who enjoyed your book to leave a review. This can be done through your email newsletter, social media, or directly in your book's back matter.
- **Use the Amazon Vine Program**: If you're selected, Amazon Vine allows trusted reviewers to receive free copies of your book in exchange for honest reviews.

Don'ts:

- **Don't Pay for Reviews**: Paying for reviews or offering incentives for positive reviews is against Amazon's policies and can result in penalties.
- **Don't Create Fake Reviews**: Posting fake reviews or asking friends and family to leave biased reviews can also lead to consequences.

Understanding Amazon's Algorithm

Amazon's algorithm, often referred to as the A9 algorithm, determines which books appear in search results and recommendations. Key factors that influence the algorithm include:

- **Sales Velocity**: The rate at which your book is selling.
- **Customer Reviews**: The number and quality of reviews your book receives.
- **Keywords**: The relevance of the keywords you use.
- **Conversion Rate**: The percentage of people who buy your book after visiting your product page.

To improve your ranking:

- **Optimize Your Listing**: Ensure your book's title, description, keywords, and categories are optimized.
- **Encourage Reviews**: Aim to get a steady stream of genuine reviews.
- **Drive Sales**: Use promotions, advertising, and other marketing strategies to boost your sales velocity.

Case Study: Navigating the Amazon Jungle Successfully

Consider the case of an indie author who successfully navigated Amazon's ecosystem. They started by optimizing their book listing with a compelling title, a detailed description, and well-researched keywords. They then enrolled their book in Kindle Unlimited, leveraging the increased visibility and page reads revenue.

To further boost their book's success, they ran targeted Sponsored Products and Lockscreen ad campaigns, continuously monitoring and adjusting their strategies. They also

Mastering Amazon Publishing

encouraged genuine reviews by engaging with their readers through email newsletters and social media. This multi-faceted approach helped the author achieve significant sales and build a loyal readership.

Navigating Amazon's complex ecosystem can be challenging, but with the right strategies and a thorough understanding of the platform, you can maximize your book's potential. Optimize your book listing, leverage Kindle Unlimited and Amazon Advertising, understand and comply with review policies, and stay informed about Amazon's algorithm. By doing so, you'll be well-equipped to succeed in the Amazon jungle.

3
Weighing the Pros and Cons

Evaluating the Benefits and Drawbacks of Amazon Publishing

Publishing on Amazon offers significant benefits but also presents some challenges. As an author, it's essential to weigh the pros and cons to make informed decisions about where and how to publish your work.

The Pros of Amazon Publishing

Global Reach and Exposure: Amazon's platform provides access to millions of readers worldwide. With its extensive network, your book can reach a global audience, increasing your potential readership significantly.

Ease of Use: Amazon's Kindle Direct Publishing (KDP) platform is user-friendly. It simplifies the self-publishing process, from manuscript upload to book cover creation and pricing.

Speed to Market: Publishing on Amazon allows for rapid publication. Once your manuscript is ready, you can have your book available for purchase in as little as 24-48 hours.

Royalty Options: Amazon offers competitive royalty rates. You can earn up to 70% royalties on eBook sales, which is higher than what many traditional publishers offer.

Mastering Amazon Publishing

Marketing Tools: Amazon provides various promotional tools such as Kindle Countdown Deals, Free Book Promotions, and Amazon Advertising. These tools help authors market their books effectively.

Print-On-Demand: With Amazon's print-on-demand service, you can offer paperback versions of your book without the need for large print runs. This minimizes upfront costs and reduces financial risk.

Customer Reviews: Amazon's customer review system can boost your book's credibility and visibility. Positive reviews can drive more sales and improve your book's ranking in search results.

The Cons of Amazon Publishing

Exclusivity Requirements: To participate in programs like Kindle Unlimited and KDP Select, you must publish exclusively on Amazon. This limits your ability to distribute your eBook on other platforms like Apple Books, Kobo, or Google Play Books.

Algorithm Dependency: Amazon's recommendation and ranking algorithms significantly impact your book's visibility. If your book doesn't perform well initially, it may struggle to gain traction.

Competitive Market: The sheer volume of books available on Amazon makes it a highly competitive marketplace. Standing out requires effective marketing and often, financial investment in advertising.

Control Over Pricing and Discounts: While you have control over your book's pricing, Amazon's pricing policies can sometimes limit your flexibility. For example, to receive the 70% royalty rate, your eBook must be priced within a certain range.

Review Policies: Amazon's strict review policies can sometimes lead to the removal of legitimate reviews. This can affect your book's overall rating and credibility.

Revenue Fluctuations: Earnings from Kindle Unlimited are based on the number of pages read, and the payment per page can fluctuate. This makes it challenging to predict your monthly income.

Print Distribution Limitations: While Amazon's print-on-demand service is convenient, it may not offer the same quality or distribution reach as traditional print publishers. Some bookstores are reluctant to stock books printed through Amazon.

Case Study: An Author's Journey Through Amazon Publishing

Consider the case of an indie author who weighed the pros and cons of Amazon publishing. Initially, they appreciated the ease of use and the rapid publication process. Their eBook gained some traction through Kindle Unlimited, benefiting from Amazon's extensive reach.

However, the author also faced challenges. The exclusivity requirement prevented them from exploring other eBook platforms, and they had to invest heavily in Amazon Advertising to maintain visibility in the competitive market. Despite these challenges, the author leveraged Amazon's marketing tools and customer reviews to build a loyal readership.

Mastering Amazon Publishing

Eventually, the author decided to diversify their distribution by releasing future books on multiple platforms. This strategy allowed them to reach new audiences and reduce dependency on Amazon's algorithms and policies.

Weighing the pros and cons of Amazon publishing is crucial for making informed decisions about your author journey. While Amazon offers significant advantages in terms of reach, ease of use, and marketing tools, it also presents challenges such as exclusivity requirements, algorithm dependency, and competitive pressures. By understanding these factors, you can better navigate the publishing landscape and make choices that align with your goals and aspirations as an author.

4
Royalties in the eBook World

Understanding eBook Royalty Structures and Their Implications

Royalties are a critical aspect of an author's income from book sales. Understanding how royalties work, especially in the eBook world, can help you make informed decisions about pricing and distribution.

Amazon's Royalty Options

Amazon offers two primary royalty options for eBooks: 35% and 70%. The royalty rate you choose affects your book's pricing and availability in different regions.

35% Royalty Option:

- **Pricing Flexibility**: You can price your eBook between $0.99 and $200.00.
- **Availability**: Your book is available worldwide without any specific requirements.
- **Delivery Costs**: You don't pay delivery costs, which can be beneficial for larger eBooks.

70% Royalty Option:

- **Pricing Requirements**: Your eBook must be priced between $2.99 and $9.99.

Mastering Amazon Publishing

- **Availability**: Your book must be available in all territories where Amazon sells eBooks.
- **Delivery Costs**: A delivery fee, based on file size, is deducted from your royalties.

Comparing Amazon with Other Platforms

Different eBook platforms offer varying royalty structures. Here's a comparison of Amazon with other popular eBook retailers:

Apple Books:

- **Royalty Rate**: 70% for eBooks priced between $0.99 and $199.99.
- **Delivery Costs**: No delivery fees.
- **Global Reach**: Extensive reach, especially in the Apple ecosystem.

Kobo:

- **Royalty Rate**: 70% for eBooks priced between $2.99 and $12.99; 45% for other prices.
- **Delivery Costs**: No delivery fees.
- **Global Reach**: Strong presence in Canada, Europe, and Asia.

Google Play Books:

- **Royalty Rate**: 70% for most books, regardless of price.
- **Delivery Costs**: No delivery fees.
- **Global Reach**: Integrated with Google's vast ecosystem.

Maximizing Your Royalties

To maximize your royalties, consider the following strategies:

Optimal Pricing: Price your eBook within the range that maximizes your royalty rate while remaining attractive to readers. For Amazon, this typically means pricing between $2.99 and $9.99.

Global Distribution: Ensure your book is available in as many regions as possible. This can increase your potential readership and sales.

Monitor and Adjust: Regularly review your sales data and adjust your pricing and marketing strategies accordingly. Experiment with different price points to see what works best for your audience.

Promotions and Discounts: Use promotional tools like Kindle Countdown Deals and Free Book Promotions to boost sales and visibility. While these promotions temporarily reduce your royalties, they can lead to increased sales and reader engagement in the long term.

Case Study: Maximizing Royalties through Strategic Pricing

An indie author published their eBook on multiple platforms, including Amazon, Apple Books, and Kobo. They initially priced their book at $4.99, taking advantage of Amazon's 70% royalty rate. After analyzing their sales data, they noticed a drop in sales after the initial launch period.

To boost sales, the author experimented with different pricing strategies. They temporarily lowered the price to $2.99 for a limited-time promotion, which resulted in a significant increase in sales and reader reviews. They also used Kindle Countdown Deals to create urgency and attract more readers.

Mastering Amazon Publishing

By monitoring their sales data and adjusting their pricing strategy, the author was able to maximize their royalties and maintain a steady stream of income from their eBook sales.

Understanding eBook royalties and how to maximize them is crucial for any author. By choosing the right royalty option, pricing your book strategically, and leveraging promotional tools, you can optimize your earnings and reach a broader audience. Comparing royalty structures across different platforms can also help you make informed decisions about where to publish your eBook. With a well-thought-out strategy, you can maximize your royalties and achieve long-term success in the eBook market.

5
Navigating the Shifting Sands

Adapting to Amazon's Constant Policy Changes

Amazon's platform is dynamic, with frequent updates and changes to its policies and algorithms. For authors, staying informed and adaptable is crucial to maintaining and growing their book's success on Amazon.

Understanding Policy Changes

Amazon regularly updates its policies related to publishing, reviews, royalties, and advertising. These changes can impact how your book is displayed, promoted, and sold. It's essential to stay informed about these updates to ensure your book complies with Amazon's guidelines and takes advantage of new opportunities.

Recent Policy Changes:

- **Review Policies**: Stricter guidelines to combat fake reviews and manipulation.
- **Advertising Rules**: Updates to how ads are displayed and the types of ads available.
- **Royalty Adjustments**: Changes in royalty structures or delivery costs.

Mastering Amazon Publishing

Staying Informed

To keep up with Amazon's policy changes:

- **Subscribe to Amazon's Newsletters**: Amazon often communicates updates through newsletters and emails.
- **Join Author Communities**: Engage with other authors on forums, social media groups, and platforms like KBoards and the Alliance of Independent Authors (ALLi). These communities often share insights and updates about Amazon's policies.
- **Follow Industry Blogs and Podcasts**: Many publishing industry blogs and podcasts discuss the latest changes and trends in the self-publishing world.

Adapting Your Strategy

When Amazon updates its policies, it's crucial to adapt your strategy accordingly. Here's how you can stay flexible and responsive:

Review and Adjust Your Listings: Ensure your book listings comply with the latest policies. Update your book descriptions, keywords, and categories as needed.

Monitor Your Advertising Campaigns: Regularly review your ad performance and make adjustments based on new rules and best practices. Experiment with different ad types and keywords to find what works best.

Engage with Your Readers: Encourage genuine reviews and interactions with your readers. Stay transparent and honest in your communication to build trust and comply with Amazon's review policies.

Case Study: Adapting to Policy Changes Successfully

An indie author noticed a sudden drop in their book's visibility and sales. After investigating, they realized that Amazon had updated its algorithm, affecting how books were ranked in search results.

To adapt, the author revisited their book's keywords and categories, ensuring they were relevant and competitive. They also increased their engagement with readers, encouraging genuine reviews through their email newsletter and social media channels.

Additionally, the author revamped their advertising strategy. They experimented with Sponsored Brands ads and adjusted their budget to focus on the most effective keywords. These changes helped the author regain visibility and boost sales, demonstrating the importance of staying adaptable in a shifting landscape.

Navigating Amazon's constant policy changes requires vigilance and adaptability. By staying informed, engaging with the author community, and being willing to adjust your strategies, you can ensure your book continues to thrive on Amazon's platform. Flexibility and responsiveness are key to maintaining and growing your book's success in the ever-evolving world of self-publishing.

6
The Amazon Conundrum

Balancing Dependence on Amazon with Diversification

Amazon provides a powerful platform for authors, but relying solely on it can be risky. Diversifying your distribution and marketing strategies can help mitigate these risks and ensure long-term success.

The Risks of Overdependence

Relying heavily on Amazon can lead to several potential risks:

- **Algorithm Changes**: Sudden changes in Amazon's algorithm can significantly impact your book's visibility and sales.
- **Policy Updates**: New policies or stricter enforcement of existing ones can affect your book's ranking, reviews, and overall performance.
- **Market Saturation**: The high volume of books on Amazon makes it a highly competitive marketplace. It can be challenging to stand out, especially if you're solely focused on Amazon.

Benefits of Diversification

Diversifying your distribution and marketing efforts can provide several benefits:

- **Broader Reach**: By making your book available on multiple platforms, you can reach a wider audience and cater to different reader preferences.
- **Reduced Risk**: Diversification helps mitigate the risks associated with changes in Amazon's policies or algorithms.
- **Increased Revenue**: Multiple revenue streams from different platforms can enhance your overall income and financial stability.

Strategies for Diversification

Distribute on Multiple Platforms: Consider publishing your book on other eBook retailers like Apple Books, Barnes & Noble Nook, Kobo, and Google Play Books. Each platform has its own audience, and expanding your reach can increase your potential readership.

Use Print-On-Demand Services: Utilize print-on-demand services like IngramSpark or Blurb to make your book available in physical form. This allows you to cater to readers who prefer print books and can help you get your book into local bookstores and libraries.

Audiobook Production: Create an audiobook version of your book using platforms like Audible's ACX or Findaway Voices. Audiobooks are a growing market and can provide an additional revenue stream.

Direct Sales and Website: Sell your books directly through your website. This gives you more control over pricing, customer data, and marketing. Use tools like Shopify or WooCommerce to set up an online store.

Mastering Amazon Publishing

Engage with Independent Bookstores: Reach out to independent bookstores to carry your book. Participate in local author events and signings to build a community presence and engage with readers directly.

Case Study: Diversification Leading to Success

An indie author initially published exclusively on Amazon and experienced moderate success. However, they recognized the risks of overdependence and decided to diversify their distribution strategy.

The author expanded their eBook distribution to include Apple Books, Kobo, and Google Play Books. They also used IngramSpark to create a print-on-demand version of their book, which allowed them to get their book into local bookstores and libraries.

Additionally, the author produced an audiobook version through Findaway Voices, tapping into the growing audiobook market. They also set up a website to sell their books directly, offering special editions and signed copies.

These diversification efforts paid off. The author saw increased sales, reduced their reliance on Amazon, and built a broader, more engaged readership. Their overall revenue grew, and they were better positioned to handle any changes in Amazon's policies or algorithms.

While Amazon provides significant opportunities for authors, overreliance on a single platform can be risky. Diversifying your distribution and marketing strategies can help mitigate these risks, increase your reach, and ensure long-term success. By expanding to multiple platforms, utilizing print-on-demand and audiobook services, and engaging with independent bookstores, you can build a more resilient and prosperous author career.

7
Navigating Amazon's Review Policies

Encouraging Genuine Reviews and Complying with Guidelines

Reviews play a crucial role in the success of your book on Amazon. They influence potential readers' buying decisions and affect your book's ranking in search results. Understanding Amazon's review policies and encouraging genuine reviews is essential for maintaining credibility and boosting sales.

Understanding Amazon's Review Policies

Amazon has strict guidelines to ensure the authenticity and reliability of customer reviews. Violating these policies can lead to the removal of reviews or even account suspension.

Key Policies:

- **No Paid Reviews**: Paying for reviews or offering incentives for positive reviews is strictly prohibited.
- **No Review Swapping**: Engaging in review swaps with other authors is against Amazon's policies.
- **Family and Friends**: Reviews from close family members and friends are generally not allowed, as they are considered biased.
- **Verified Purchase Reviews**: Reviews from verified purchases carry more weight and credibility.

Encouraging Genuine Reviews

To gather genuine reviews, consider the following strategies:

Ask Your Readers: Politely ask readers to leave a review if they enjoyed your book. You can include a request at the end of your book, in your email newsletter, or on your social media channels.

Engage with Your Audience: Build a relationship with your readers through social media, email newsletters, and author websites. Engaged readers are more likely to leave reviews.

Use Amazon's Programs: If eligible, participate in Amazon's Vine Program, which provides free copies of your book to trusted reviewers in exchange for honest reviews.

Book Review Services: While paying for reviews is not allowed, you can use legitimate book review services that comply with Amazon's policies. These services often send review copies to potential reviewers without guaranteeing a positive review.

Advanced Review Copies (ARCs): Send ARCs to book bloggers, influencers, and reviewers before your book's release. This can help generate buzz and gather reviews early on.

Managing and Responding to Reviews

Monitor Reviews: Regularly check your reviews to understand reader feedback. This can provide valuable insights into what readers like and areas for improvement.

Mastering Amazon Publishing

Respond Professionally: Respond to reviews professionally and courteously, especially negative ones. Thank reviewers for their feedback and address any concerns constructively.

Report Violations: If you notice any reviews that violate Amazon's policies, report them through Amazon's review reporting system.

Case Study: Building Credibility Through Genuine Reviews

An indie author published a thriller novel on Amazon and understood the importance of genuine reviews for building credibility and boosting sales. They implemented several strategies to encourage reviews:

- **Email Newsletter**: The author built an email list of engaged readers and sent out newsletters asking for reviews.
- **Social Media Engagement**: They actively engaged with readers on social media, creating a loyal community that was eager to support their work.
- **Advanced Review Copies**: The author sent ARCs to book bloggers and reviewers, resulting in early reviews and increased visibility.

As reviews started to come in, the author monitored and responded to them professionally. They thanked reviewers for positive feedback and addressed any constructive criticism with grace. This approach helped the author build a solid reputation, leading to more sales and a growing reader base.

Navigating Amazon's review policies and encouraging genuine reviews is crucial for the success of your book. By understanding and complying with Amazon's guidelines, asking readers for reviews, engaging with your audience, and using legitimate review services, you can build credibility and boost your book's visibility. Professional management of reviews, including responding to feedback and reporting violations, will help maintain your book's reputation and drive long-term success.

8
Navigating Algorithm Dependency on Amazon

Optimizing Your Book's Visibility and Sales

Amazon's algorithm plays a significant role in determining your book's visibility and sales. Understanding how the algorithm works and optimizing your book's listing accordingly can help you achieve better rankings and attract more readers.

How Amazon's Algorithm Works

Amazon's algorithm, often referred to as the A9 algorithm, determines which books appear in search results, recommendations, and various lists. Several factors influence the algorithm, including:

- **Sales Velocity**: The rate at which your book is selling. Consistent sales over time can boost your ranking.
- **Customer Reviews**: The number and quality of reviews your book receives. Positive reviews can improve your visibility.
- **Keywords**: The relevance of the keywords you use in your book's title, subtitle, and description.
- **Conversion Rate**: The percentage of people who purchase your book after visiting your product page.
- **Click-Through Rate (CTR)**: The percentage of people who click on your book's listing when it appears in search results or recommendations.

Optimizing Your Book Listing

To optimize your book listing for Amazon's algorithm, consider the following strategies:

Title and Subtitle: Use relevant keywords in your book's title and subtitle. Make sure they are compelling and accurately reflect your book's content.

Book Description: Write a persuasive and engaging book description. Use HTML formatting to make it visually appealing and include relevant keywords.

Categories: Choose appropriate categories for your book. Aim for categories that are relevant but not overly competitive. You can request additional categories by contacting Amazon support.

Keywords: Research and select keywords that potential readers are likely to search for. Use tools like Amazon's Keyword Planner, Publisher Rocket, and Google Keyword Planner to find high-volume, relevant keywords.

Cover Design: A professional and eye-catching cover can significantly impact your book's CTR. Invest in a high-quality cover that appeals to your target audience.

Pricing: Set a competitive price for your book. Experiment with different price points to see what works best for your audience.

Mastering Amazon Publishing

Driving Sales and Reviews

Consistent sales and positive reviews are crucial for improving your book's ranking. Here are some strategies to boost sales and gather reviews:

Promotions and Discounts: Use promotional tools like Kindle Countdown Deals and Free Book Promotions to attract more readers and drive sales.

Amazon Advertising: Run targeted ad campaigns using Sponsored Products, Sponsored Brands, and Lockscreen Ads. Monitor and adjust your campaigns to optimize performance.

Email Marketing: Build and engage with your email list. Use newsletters to announce promotions, new releases, and ask for reviews.

Social Media Marketing: Leverage social media platforms to connect with your audience, share updates, and promote your book.

Book Launch Strategy: Plan a well-executed book launch to generate buzz and drive initial sales. Use a combination of email marketing, social media, and advertising to maximize your book's visibility.

Case Study: Optimizing for Algorithm Success

An indie author published a mystery novel on Amazon and wanted to optimize their book's visibility. They started by researching and selecting relevant keywords for their title, subtitle, and book description. They also invested in a professional cover design that resonated with their target audience.

The author ran a series of Kindle Countdown Deals to boost sales and used Amazon Advertising to target specific keywords. They engaged with their email list and social media followers, asking for reviews and promoting the book.

As a result, the book's sales velocity increased, leading to higher rankings in Amazon's search results and recommendations. The author also saw a steady stream of positive reviews, further improving their book's visibility and credibility.

Navigating algorithm dependency on Amazon requires a strategic approach to optimizing your book's listing and driving sales and reviews. By understanding how the algorithm works and implementing best practices for keywords, categories, cover design, and pricing, you can improve your book's visibility and attract more readers. Consistent sales, positive reviews, and effective marketing strategies are key to achieving long-term success on Amazon's platform.

Mastering Amazon Publishing

9
Weighing the Pros and Cons of Amazon's KDP Select Exclusivity Period

Evaluating the Benefits and Trade-offs of KDP Select

Amazon's KDP Select program offers several benefits to authors, but it also comes with the trade-off of exclusivity. Understanding the pros and cons of enrolling in KDP Select can help you decide if it's the right choice for your book.

Benefits of KDP Select

Kindle Unlimited (KU) and Kindle Owners' Lending Library (KOLL): By enrolling in KDP Select, your book becomes available to millions of Kindle Unlimited subscribers and Kindle Owners' Lending Library users. This can significantly increase your book's exposure and readership.

Higher Royalties in Select Regions: For books enrolled in KDP Select, Amazon offers a 70% royalty rate for sales in certain regions, such as Brazil, Japan, India, and Mexico. This can boost your earnings from international sales.

Promotional Tools: KDP Select provides access to promotional tools like Kindle Countdown Deals and Free Book Promotions. These tools can help you attract new readers, boost sales, and improve your book's ranking.

Page Reads Revenue: In addition to royalties from sales, you can earn money based on the number of pages read by Kindle Unlimited subscribers. This provides an additional revenue stream and can be particularly lucrative for longer books.

Trade-offs of KDP Select

Exclusivity Requirement: To participate in KDP Select, you must agree to make your eBook exclusive to Amazon for a 90-day period. This means you cannot sell your eBook on other platforms like Apple Books, Barnes & Noble Nook, Kobo, or Google Play Books during this time.

Reduced Distribution: Exclusivity limits your book's distribution, potentially reducing your overall reach and readership. Readers who prefer other eBook platforms may not have access to your book.

Dependency on Amazon: Enrolling in KDP Select increases your dependency on Amazon's platform. Changes in Amazon's policies, algorithms, or royalty structures can have a significant impact on your earnings and visibility.

Evaluating the Decision

To determine if KDP Select is right for your book, consider the following factors:

Genre and Audience: Some genres perform particularly well on Kindle Unlimited, such as romance, mystery, and science fiction. If your book fits into one of these genres, KDP Select may be beneficial.

Mastering Amazon Publishing

Marketing Strategy: If you plan to leverage Amazon's promotional tools and focus on building a strong presence on Amazon, KDP Select can provide valuable resources.

Revenue Goals: Evaluate your revenue goals and consider if the potential earnings from page reads and higher royalties in select regions outweigh the trade-offs of reduced distribution.

Case Study: Success with KDP Select

An indie author published a romance novel and decided to enroll in KDP Select. They leveraged Kindle Unlimited to reach a larger audience and used Kindle Countdown Deals to drive sales during promotional periods.

The author also focused on gathering reviews from Kindle Unlimited readers, which boosted their book's visibility and credibility. As a result, their book saw a significant increase in page reads and overall sales, making KDP Select a worthwhile choice for their marketing strategy.

However, after the initial 90-day exclusivity period, the author chose to diversify their distribution to other platforms to reach a broader audience. This balanced approach allowed them to maximize the benefits of KDP Select while also expanding their reach.

Weighing the pros and cons of Amazon's KDP Select exclusivity period is essential for making an informed decision about your book's distribution strategy. While KDP Select offers valuable benefits like Kindle Unlimited access, higher royalties, and promotional tools, it also requires exclusivity, which can limit your reach. By considering your genre, audience, marketing strategy, and revenue goals, you can determine if KDP Select is the right choice for your book.

10
Navigating the Waters of eBook Pricing

Strategies for Setting the Optimal Price for Your eBook

Setting the right price for your eBook is crucial for maximizing sales and royalties. It requires balancing competitiveness, perceived value, and market trends. In this chapter, we'll explore strategies for pricing your eBook effectively.

Understanding Pricing Tiers

Different price points can appeal to different segments of readers. Here's a breakdown of common pricing tiers and their potential impacts:

$0.99 - $2.99: This price range is attractive to bargain hunters and can lead to higher sales volume. It's often used for promotions or to attract new readers to a series.

$2.99 - $4.99: This is a popular range for indie authors, balancing affordability with higher royalty rates. It's suitable for most genres and offers a good balance between sales volume and revenue.

$5.99 - $9.99: This range positions your book as a premium product. It's often used for established authors or books with substantial content and perceived value.

$9.99 and Above: Typically reserved for traditionally published books or specialized content. It can be challenging for indie authors to achieve high sales at this price point without a strong brand or niche market.

Factors to Consider in Pricing

Genre and Competition: Research the pricing of similar books in your genre. Competitive pricing can help your book stand out, especially in a crowded market.

Length and Content: Longer books or those with substantial content (e.g., comprehensive guides, textbooks) can justify higher prices. Consider the value your book offers to readers.

Target Audience: Understand your target audience's willingness to pay. For example, readers of romance novels may be more price-sensitive than readers of specialized non-fiction.

Promotional Pricing: Use temporary price drops to boost visibility and attract new readers. Promotions like Kindle Countdown Deals and Free Book Promotions can drive sales and reviews.

Experimenting with Pricing

Don't be afraid to experiment with different price points to find what works best for your book. Monitor your sales data and make adjustments as needed. Here are some strategies for experimenting with pricing:

Mastering Amazon Publishing

Introductory Pricing: Launch your book at a lower price to attract early readers and reviews. Gradually increase the price as your book gains traction.

Seasonal Promotions: Align price drops with holidays, special events, or book anniversaries to attract attention and boost sales.

Series Pricing: If you have a series, consider pricing the first book lower to entice readers, then set higher prices for subsequent books.

Case Study: Effective Pricing Strategies

An indie author published a thriller novel and initially priced it at $2.99. They ran a Kindle Countdown Deal, dropping the price to $0.99 for a week. The promotion resulted in a significant increase in sales and visibility, helping the book climb the charts.

After the promotion, the author raised the price to $3.99. This new price point balanced affordability with higher royalties, maintaining steady sales and maximizing revenue. By experimenting with different pricing strategies, the author found the optimal price for their book.

Navigating the waters of eBook pricing requires careful consideration of various factors, including genre, competition, content, and target audience. By understanding different pricing tiers, experimenting with price points, and using promotional strategies, you can set the optimal price for your eBook. Effective pricing can enhance your book's visibility, attract more readers, and maximize your royalties.

B Alan Bourgeois

Mastering Amazon Publishing

Section 2
Amazon Advantage
Your Path to Publishing Success

Contents

14. The Global Reach of Amazon	58
15. The Ease of Self-Publishing with Amazon's	
16. KDP Platform	62
17. Empowering Authors Retaining Control with Amazon KDP	66
18. Maximizing Profits Amazon's Competitive eBook	
19. Royalties For Authors	70
20. Rapid Results: Quick eBook and Paperback	
21. Publishing with Amazon KDP	74
22. Amplify Your Reach: Amazon Advertising for Authors	79
23. Unleash Your Earnings: Kindle Unlimited for Authors	83
24. The Power of Print-On-Demand	87
25. Harnessing the Power of Customer Reviews	91
26. Amazon Author Central	95
About the Author	99
Other Books by the Author in this Series	100

1
The Global Reach of Amazon

Leveraging Amazon's International Markets

Amazon's global presence provides authors with the opportunity to reach readers worldwide. Understanding how to navigate and leverage international markets can significantly expand your book's reach and boost sales.

Amazon's International Marketplaces

Amazon operates in numerous countries, including the United States, Canada, the United Kingdom, Germany, France, Italy, Spain, Japan, India, and more. Each marketplace has its own unique audience and preferences.

Key Marketplaces:

- **Amazon.com**: The largest and most competitive marketplace, serving the United States and international customers.
- **Amazon.co.uk**: A significant market for English-language books, serving the United Kingdom.
- **Amazon.de**: Germany's marketplace, one of the largest non-English speaking markets.

- **Amazon.co.jp**: Japan's marketplace, with a strong eBook market.
- **Amazon.in**: India's rapidly growing market, with increasing demand for English-language books.

Localization Strategies

To effectively reach international readers, consider the following localization strategies:

Translation: Translate your book into the local language to reach a broader audience. This can be particularly effective for large markets like Germany, France, and Japan.

Localized Keywords and Categories: Research and use relevant keywords and categories for each marketplace. This can improve your book's visibility in local search results.

Cultural Sensitivity: Be mindful of cultural differences and preferences. Tailor your book's content, cover, and marketing messages to resonate with local readers.

Pricing Adjustments: Set prices that are competitive and appropriate for each market. Consider local purchasing power and pricing trends.

Marketing to International Readers

Amazon Advertising: Use Amazon Advertising to target specific international markets. Create ad campaigns in different languages to reach non-English speaking audiences.

International Book Launches: Plan book launches tailored to specific markets. Coordinate promotions, reviews, and marketing efforts to coincide with local holidays and events.

Mastering Amazon Publishing

Social Media and Influencers: Engage with local readers through social media platforms popular in each country. Collaborate with local book bloggers and influencers to promote your book.

Global Reviews: Encourage reviews from international readers. Positive reviews in local languages can enhance your book's credibility and attract more readers.

Case Study: Expanding Reach through Localization

An indie author published a mystery novel and decided to expand their reach to international markets. They translated the book into German and launched it on Amazon.de.

To promote the German edition, the author ran Amazon Advertising campaigns targeting German readers. They also collaborated with local book bloggers and influencers to generate buzz.

The author researched and used relevant German keywords and categories, improving the book's visibility in local search results. They also set a competitive price that appealed to German readers.

As a result, the book saw a significant increase in sales and positive reviews from German readers. The author successfully expanded their reach and built a loyal international audience.

Leveraging Amazon's international markets can significantly expand your book's reach and boost sales. By localizing your book through translation, using relevant keywords and categories, and tailoring your marketing efforts to specific markets, you can effectively reach readers worldwide. Understanding and engaging with international audiences is key to achieving global success in the self-publishing world.

2
The Ease of Self-Publishing with Amazon's KDP Platform

A Step-by-Step Guide to Publishing Your Book on KDP

Amazon's Kindle Direct Publishing (KDP) platform offers a user-friendly and efficient way for authors to self-publish their books. This chapter provides a step-by-step guide to navigating the KDP platform and publishing your book.

Setting Up Your KDP Account

Create an Amazon Account: If you don't already have an Amazon account, create one. You'll use this account to access the KDP platform.

Sign Up for KDP: Visit the Kindle Direct Publishing website and sign in with your Amazon account. Complete the KDP registration process by providing the required information.

Set Up Your Author Profile: Create an author profile on Amazon Author Central. This profile allows you to manage your author page, track book sales, and interact with readers.

Preparing Your Manuscript

Formatting Your Manuscript: Ensure your manuscript is properly formatted for eBook publication. Use tools like Kindle Create or professional formatting services to create a polished, reader-friendly eBook.

Creating a Cover: Design a professional and eye-catching cover for your book. You can use tools like Canva, hire a professional designer, or use Amazon's Cover Creator tool.

Writing a Book Description: Craft a compelling and informative book description. Use relevant keywords and HTML formatting to make your description engaging and visually appealing.

Choosing Keywords and Categories: Research and select keywords and categories that are relevant to your book. These will help improve your book's visibility in Amazon's search results.

Publishing Your Book

Upload Your Manuscript and Cover: Sign in to your KDP account and click on "Create a New Title." Follow the prompts to upload your manuscript and cover file.

Enter Book Details: Provide all the necessary details about your book, including the title, subtitle, author name, and book description. Select the appropriate keywords and categories.

Set Your Pricing and Royalties: Choose your book's pricing and royalty options. Decide whether to enroll in KDP Select,

Mastering Amazon Publishing

which offers additional promotional benefits in exchange for exclusivity.

Preview Your Book: Use the online previewer to review your book's formatting and appearance. Make any necessary adjustments before publishing.

Publish Your Book: Once you're satisfied with all the details, click "Publish Your Kindle eBook." Your book will be reviewed by Amazon and typically becomes available for purchase within 24-48 hours.

Promoting Your Book

Launch Strategy: Plan a book launch to generate excitement and drive initial sales. Use your email list, social media, and author website to announce the launch.

Amazon Advertising: Create ad campaigns to promote your book on Amazon. Use Sponsored Products, Sponsored Brands, and Lockscreen Ads to reach your target audience.

Social Media Marketing: Leverage social media platforms to engage with readers and promote your book. Share updates, behind-the-scenes content, and promotional offers.

Gathering Reviews: Encourage readers to leave reviews on your book's Amazon page. Positive reviews can boost your book's visibility and credibility.

Case Study: A Smooth Publishing Experience with KDP

An indie author published their first science fiction novel using KDP. They followed the step-by-step process to format their manuscript, create a compelling cover, and write an engaging book description.

The author researched relevant keywords and categories to improve their book's visibility. They set a competitive price and chose the 70% royalty option.

After publishing, the author promoted their book through a well-planned launch strategy, including social media marketing and Amazon Advertising. They also encouraged early readers to leave reviews.

The book quickly gained traction, receiving positive reviews and climbing the charts in its category. The author's smooth experience with KDP highlighted the platform's ease of use and effectiveness for self-publishing.

Amazon's KDP platform provides a straightforward and efficient way for authors to self-publish their books. By following a step-by-step process, from setting up your account to promoting your book, you can successfully navigate the platform and reach a global audience. The ease of self-publishing with KDP makes it an attractive option for authors looking to bring their work to market quickly and effectively.

3
Empowering Authors
Retaining Control with Amazon KDP

Maintaining Creative and Financial Control Over Your Work

One of the significant advantages of self-publishing with Amazon KDP is the ability to retain control over your creative and financial decisions. This chapter explores how KDP empowers authors to maintain control and make strategic choices for their books.

Creative Control

Content and Editing: As a self-published author, you have complete control over your book's content. You can choose your editor, make revisions, and decide on the final version of your manuscript.

Cover Design: You can create or commission a cover that reflects your vision and appeals to your target audience. This creative freedom allows you to make your book stand out.

Book Layout: You have the flexibility to design your book's layout, including font choices, chapter headings, and interior formatting. This ensures that your book aligns with your artistic vision.

Title and Subtitle: You can choose a title and subtitle that best represent your book and attract potential readers. This is crucial for marketing and branding purposes.

Financial Control

Pricing: You have the authority to set your book's price, allowing you to experiment with different price points and promotional strategies. This control helps you optimize your royalties and sales.

Royalties: KDP offers competitive royalty options, with up to 70% royalties on eBook sales. This provides a significant financial incentive compared to traditional publishing.

Promotion and Marketing: You can decide on your marketing and promotional strategies. This includes running ads, organizing book launches, and leveraging social media to reach your audience.

Distribution: While enrolling in KDP Select requires exclusivity, you can choose to distribute your book on multiple platforms if you opt out. This flexibility allows you to reach a broader audience.

Making Informed Decisions

Market Research: Conduct thorough market research to understand your genre, target audience, and competition. Use this information to make informed decisions about your book's content, pricing, and marketing.

Mastering Amazon Publishing

Experimentation: Don't be afraid to experiment with different strategies. Test various price points, promotional campaigns, and marketing techniques to find what works best for your book.

Tracking and Analytics: Use KDP's analytics tools to track your book's performance. Monitor sales data, customer reviews, and ad performance to make data-driven decisions.

Case Study: Empowering Success Through Control

An indie author published a fantasy novel on KDP, valuing the creative and financial control the platform offered. They worked closely with an editor to refine their manuscript and hired a professional designer to create a captivating cover.

The author set an initial price of $3.99, which they adjusted based on sales data and reader feedback. They also ran targeted Amazon Advertising campaigns to boost visibility.

By retaining control over their marketing strategy, the author organized a successful book launch, leveraging social media and email newsletters to engage with readers. This strategic approach led to strong sales, positive reviews, and a growing fan base.

The author's ability to make informed decisions and retain control over their book's production and marketing was crucial to their success.

Amazon KDP empowers authors by providing creative and financial control over their work. This control allows you to make strategic decisions about your book's content, pricing, and marketing, leading to a more personalized and potentially successful publishing experience. By conducting market research, experimenting with different strategies, and using KDP's analytics tools, you can optimize your book's performance and achieve your publishing goals.

4
Maximizing Profits
Amazon's Competitive eBook Royalties for Authors

Leveraging Amazon's Royalty Structures to Increase Earnings

Amazon's Kindle Direct Publishing (KDP) platform offers competitive royalty options that can significantly impact an author's earnings. This chapter explores how to maximize your profits by understanding and leveraging Amazon's eBook royalty structures.

Understanding Amazon's Royalty Options

Amazon offers two primary royalty options for eBooks: 35% and 70%. Each option has specific requirements and implications for your earnings.

35% Royalty Option:

- **Pricing Flexibility**: You can price your eBook between $0.99 and $200.00.
- **Availability**: Your book is available worldwide without any specific requirements.
- **Delivery Costs**: You don't pay delivery costs, which can be beneficial for larger eBooks.

70% Royalty Option:

- **Pricing Requirements**: Your eBook must be priced between $2.99 and $9.99.
- **Availability**: Your book must be available in all territories where Amazon sells eBooks.
- **Delivery Costs**: A delivery fee, based on file size, is deducted from your royalties.

Choosing the Right Royalty Option

To choose the right royalty option for your book, consider the following factors:

Book Length and File Size: If your eBook is large and has high delivery costs, the 35% royalty option might be more beneficial. For standard-length books, the 70% option usually provides higher earnings.

Pricing Strategy: If you plan to price your book below $2.99 or above $9.99, the 35% royalty option is your only choice. For books priced within the $2.99 to $9.99 range, the 70% option is more lucrative.

International Sales: The 70% royalty option requires your book to be available in all territories. If you're targeting a global audience, this option is advantageous.

Maximizing Your Royalties

Optimal Pricing: Price your eBook within the range that maximizes your royalty rate while remaining attractive to readers. For Amazon, this typically means pricing between $2.99 and $9.99.

KDP Select Enrollment: Consider enrolling in KDP Select, which offers additional promotional tools and opportunities to earn through Kindle Unlimited page reads. However, remember that this requires exclusivity.

Promotional Strategies: Use Kindle Countdown Deals and Free Book Promotions to boost sales and visibility. These promotions can lead to increased royalties in the long term.

International Pricing: Adjust your book's price for different regions to account for local purchasing power and market conditions. This can enhance your book's competitiveness and sales in international markets.

Monitoring and Adjusting: Regularly review your sales data and adjust your pricing and marketing strategies accordingly. Experiment with different price points and promotions to find what works best for your book.

Case Study: Maximizing Royalties with Strategic Pricing

An indie author published a self-help book on Amazon and aimed to maximize their royalties. They initially priced the book at $4.99, leveraging the 70% royalty option.

The author enrolled in KDP Select, utilizing Kindle Countdown Deals and Free Book Promotions to boost visibility and attract new readers. These promotions resulted in a significant increase in sales and reviews.

To optimize international sales, the author adjusted the book's price for different regions, making it more competitive in local markets. This strategy led to higher overall royalties and a broader global readership.

By monitoring sales data and experimenting with different pricing strategies, the author maximized their earnings and achieved sustained success on Amazon.

Maximizing your profits on Amazon requires a thorough understanding of the platform's royalty options and strategic pricing. By choosing the right royalty option, leveraging KDP Select, implementing effective promotional strategies, and optimizing international pricing, you can significantly increase your earnings. Regularly reviewing your sales data and adjusting your strategies will help you stay competitive and achieve long-term success in the eBook market.

5
Rapid Results: Quick eBook and Paperback Publishing with Amazon KDP

Streamlining the Publishing Process for Faster Results

Amazon's Kindle Direct Publishing (KDP) platform allows authors to publish eBooks and paperbacks quickly and efficiently. This chapter explores how to streamline the publishing process to achieve rapid results and bring your book to market swiftly.

Preparing Your Manuscript

Editing and Proofreading: Ensure your manuscript is thoroughly edited and proofread. This is crucial for maintaining quality and credibility. Consider hiring professional editors or using editing software to refine your work.

Formatting: Proper formatting is essential for both eBooks and paperbacks. Use tools like Kindle Create for eBooks and professional formatting services for print. Ensure your manuscript meets Amazon's formatting guidelines to avoid delays.

Cover Design: Create a professional and eye-catching cover. For paperbacks, design a full cover that includes the front, back, and spine. Use tools like Canva or hire a professional designer to ensure your cover stands out.

Metadata: Prepare your book's metadata, including the title, subtitle, author name, keywords, and categories. This information is critical for discoverability and should be carefully chosen to attract your target audience.

Publishing Your eBook

Create a New Title: Sign in to your KDP account and click on "Create a New Title." Choose the "Kindle eBook" option and follow the prompts to enter your book details.

Upload Your Manuscript and Cover: Upload your formatted manuscript and cover file. Use the online previewer to review your eBook's formatting and appearance.

Enter Book Details: Provide all the necessary details about your book, including the title, subtitle, author name, and book description. Select the appropriate keywords and categories.

Set Your Pricing and Royalties: Choose your book's pricing and royalty options. Decide whether to enroll in KDP Select, which offers additional promotional benefits in exchange for exclusivity.

Publish Your eBook: Once you're satisfied with all the details, click "Publish Your Kindle eBook." Your book will be reviewed by Amazon and typically becomes available for purchase within 24-48 hours.

Mastering Amazon Publishing

Publishing Your Paperback

Create a Paperback Version: In your KDP account, click on "Create a New Title" and choose the "Paperback" option. Enter your book details and upload your manuscript and cover file.

Preview Your Paperback: Use the print previewer to review your paperback's formatting and appearance. Make any necessary adjustments before proceeding.

Select Print Options: Choose your print options, including trim size, paper type, and cover finish. These options affect the quality and cost of your paperback.

Set Your Pricing and Distribution: Set the price for your paperback and choose your distribution channels. Amazon offers expanded distribution to reach bookstores and libraries.

Publish Your Paperback: Once you're satisfied with all the details, click "Publish Your Paperback." Your book will be reviewed by Amazon and typically becomes available for purchase within 24-48 hours.

Promoting Your Book

Launch Strategy: Plan a book launch to generate excitement and drive initial sales. Use your email list, social media, and author website to announce the launch.

Amazon Advertising: Create ad campaigns to promote your book on Amazon. Use Sponsored Products, Sponsored Brands, and Lockscreen Ads to reach your target audience.

Social Media Marketing: Leverage social media platforms to engage with readers and promote your book. Share updates, behind-the-scenes content, and promotional offers.

Gathering Reviews: Encourage readers to leave reviews on your book's Amazon page. Positive reviews can boost your book's visibility and credibility.

Case Study: Achieving Rapid Results with KDP

An indie author published a historical fiction novel and aimed to bring their book to market quickly. They followed a streamlined publishing process, ensuring their manuscript was thoroughly edited and professionally formatted.

The author used Kindle Create to format their eBook and hired a designer to create an eye-catching cover. They prepared all the necessary metadata and uploaded their manuscript and cover file to KDP.

Within 48 hours, the eBook was live on Amazon. The author simultaneously published a paperback version, using KDP's print-on-demand service to reach readers who prefer physical copies.

To promote the book, the author ran Amazon Advertising campaigns and leveraged social media to engage with readers. The rapid publication process and effective marketing strategy led to strong initial sales and positive reviews.

Amazon's KDP platform allows authors to publish eBooks and paperbacks quickly and efficiently. By following a streamlined publishing process, from preparing your manuscript to promoting your book, you can achieve rapid results and bring

Mastering Amazon Publishing

your book to market swiftly. The ease and speed of self-publishing with KDP make it an attractive option for authors looking to reach a global audience quickly and effectively.

6
Amplify Your Reach:
Amazon Advertising for Authors

Effective Strategies for Promoting Your Book on Amazon

Amazon Advertising provides powerful tools for authors to promote their books and reach a broader audience. This chapter explores effective strategies for using Amazon Advertising to amplify your book's reach and boost sales.

Types of Amazon Ads

Amazon offers several types of ads that authors can use to promote their books:

Sponsored Products: These ads appear within search results and on product detail pages. They are highly effective for targeting specific keywords and driving sales.

Sponsored Brands: These ads appear at the top of search results and include your book's cover, a custom headline, and a logo. They are great for building brand awareness and showcasing multiple books.

Lockscreen Ads: These ads appear on the lock screens of Kindle devices. They are useful for targeting avid Kindle readers and promoting eBooks.

Mastering Amazon Publishing

Sponsored Display Ads: These ads appear on and off Amazon, targeting shoppers based on their browsing behavior. They can help you reach a wider audience and drive traffic to your book's detail page.

Creating Effective Ad Campaigns

Research Keywords: Use tools like Amazon's Keyword Planner, Publisher Rocket, and Google Keyword Planner to find relevant keywords with good search volume. Choose keywords that are highly relevant to your book's content and target audience.

Set a Budget: Determine your advertising budget based on your marketing goals and financial resources. Start with a modest budget and adjust based on your campaign's performance.

Create Compelling Ad Copy: Write persuasive and engaging ad copy that highlights your book's unique selling points. Use a strong call-to-action to encourage clicks and conversions.

Design Eye-Catching Ads: For Sponsored Brands and Lockscreen Ads, use high-quality images and graphics that capture attention. Ensure your book cover is prominently displayed and visually appealing.

Target Your Audience: Use Amazon's targeting options to reach specific demographics, interests, and behaviors. Refine your targeting to focus on readers who are most likely to be interested in your book.

Monitoring and Optimizing Campaigns

Track Performance Metrics: Monitor key metrics such as impressions, clicks, conversion rate, and return on ad spend (ROAS). Use this data to assess the effectiveness of your campaigns.

Adjust Bids and Budgets: Based on your campaign's performance, adjust your bids and budgets to optimize results. Increase bids on high-performing keywords and reduce spending on underperforming ones.

Test Different Ad Variations: Experiment with different ad copy, images, and targeting options to find what works best. A/B testing can help you identify the most effective combinations.

Analyze and Refine: Regularly review your campaign data and make adjustments to improve performance. Use insights from your analysis to refine your targeting, ad copy, and bidding strategy.

Case Study: Boosting Sales with Amazon Advertising

An indie author published a thriller novel and decided to use Amazon Advertising to boost sales. They started with Sponsored Products ads, targeting relevant keywords with high search volume.

The author set a modest budget and closely monitored their campaign's performance. They adjusted their bids based on which keywords were driving the most clicks and conversions.

To increase brand awareness, the author also ran Sponsored Brands ads, showcasing their book cover and a compelling

Mastering Amazon Publishing

headline. They used eye-catching graphics to capture attention and drive traffic to their book's detail page.

By testing different ad variations and refining their targeting, the author achieved a significant increase in sales and visibility. Amazon Advertising proved to be a valuable tool for reaching a broader audience and boosting their book's success.

Amazon Advertising offers powerful tools for authors to promote their books and reach a broader audience. By creating effective ad campaigns, monitoring performance metrics, and optimizing your strategies, you can amplify your book's reach and boost sales. Leveraging Amazon's advertising platform can help you achieve your marketing goals and build a successful author brand.

7
Unleash Your Earnings: Kindle Unlimited for Authors

Maximizing Revenue with Kindle Unlimited

Kindle Unlimited (KU) is a subscription service that allows readers to access a vast library of eBooks for a monthly fee. For authors, participating in KU can provide an additional revenue stream and increase your book's exposure. This chapter explores strategies for maximizing your earnings with Kindle Unlimited.

Understanding Kindle Unlimited

How KU Works: Readers pay a monthly subscription fee to access KU's library. Authors earn money based on the number of pages read by subscribers. The total payout depends on the KU Global Fund, which Amazon allocates each month.

Eligibility and Enrollment: To participate in KU, you must enroll your book in Amazon's KDP Select program, which requires exclusivity. This means your eBook cannot be available on other platforms while enrolled in KU.

Benefits of Kindle Unlimited

Increased Visibility: KU books often receive higher visibility on Amazon, including better placement in search results and

Mastering Amazon Publishing

recommendations. This can lead to increased readership and sales.

Page Reads Revenue: Authors earn money based on the number of pages read by KU subscribers. This can be particularly lucrative for longer books and series.

Promotional Opportunities: KU participation provides access to promotional tools like Kindle Countdown Deals and Free Book Promotions, which can boost your book's visibility and attract new readers.

Engaged Readers: KU subscribers are avid readers who are more likely to discover and read your book. This can lead to increased reviews and word-of-mouth marketing.

Strategies for Maximizing KU Earnings

Write Longer Books or Series: Longer books and series can generate more page reads, increasing your KU earnings. Consider expanding your book's content or writing sequels to keep readers engaged.

Optimize Your Book Listing: Ensure your book's title, subtitle, description, keywords, and categories are optimized for Amazon's search algorithm. This will help your book appear in relevant search results and recommendations.

Leverage Promotions: Use Kindle Countdown Deals and Free Book Promotions to boost your book's visibility and attract new readers. These promotions can lead to increased page reads and reviews.

Engage with Readers: Build a loyal reader base by engaging with your audience through social media, email newsletters, and author websites. Encourage readers to leave reviews and share your book with others.

Monitor and Adjust: Regularly review your KU earnings and page reads data. Use this information to make informed decisions about your marketing and promotional strategies.

Case Study: Success with Kindle Unlimited

An indie author published a fantasy series and enrolled their books in Kindle Unlimited. They focused on writing longer books, each with engaging storylines that kept readers hooked.

To boost visibility, the author optimized their book listings with relevant keywords and compelling descriptions. They also ran Kindle Countdown Deals to attract new readers and drive sales.

The author engaged with their audience through social media and email newsletters, encouraging readers to leave reviews and share their books. This led to increased word-of-mouth marketing and a growing reader base.

By monitoring their KU earnings and page reads data, the author adjusted their promotional strategies to maximize their revenue. The combination of longer books, optimized listings, effective promotions, and reader engagement resulted in significant success with Kindle Unlimited.

Kindle Unlimited offers a valuable opportunity for authors to increase their book's exposure and generate additional revenue through page reads. By writing longer books or series, optimizing your book listing, leveraging promotional tools,

Mastering Amazon Publishing

engaging with readers, and monitoring your earnings, you can maximize your success with Kindle Unlimited. Participating in KU can help you reach a broader audience and achieve your financial goals as an author.

8
The Power of Print-On-Demand

Leveraging Print-On-Demand Services to Expand Your Reach

Print-On-Demand (POD) services provide authors with a cost-effective way to offer physical copies of their books without the need for large print runs. This chapter explores the benefits of POD and how to leverage these services to expand your reach and boost sales.

Understanding Print-On-Demand

How POD Works: With POD, books are printed individually as orders come in, eliminating the need for large print runs and inventory storage. This allows authors to offer physical copies without significant upfront costs.

Popular POD Services: Amazon's KDP Print and IngramSpark are two of the most popular POD services. Each offers unique features and distribution options that can benefit authors.

Amazon KDP Print: Integrates seamlessly with your KDP account, making it easy to publish both eBooks and paperbacks. Offers expanded distribution to reach bookstores and libraries.

IngramSpark: Provides broader distribution options, including access to a global network of bookstores, libraries, and online

Mastering Amazon Publishing

retailers. Known for high-quality printing and more customization options.

Benefits of Print-On-Demand

Cost-Effective: POD eliminates the need for large print runs and inventory storage, reducing upfront costs and financial risk.

No Inventory Management: Books are printed as orders come in, eliminating the need to manage inventory and handle shipping logistics.

High-Quality Printing: POD services offer professional-quality printing, ensuring that your book looks polished and appealing to readers.

Expanded Distribution: POD services like IngramSpark provide access to a global distribution network, helping you reach more readers and increase sales.

Flexibility and Control: POD allows you to make updates and changes to your book without the need for reprinting large quantities. This flexibility ensures that your book stays current and accurate.

Leveraging POD for Success

Choosing the Right POD Service: Consider your distribution goals and choose the POD service that best meets your needs. Amazon KDP Print is ideal for seamless integration with your KDP account, while IngramSpark offers broader distribution options.

Formatting for Print: Ensure your manuscript is properly formatted for print. This includes selecting the appropriate trim size, margins, font, and layout. Use professional formatting services if needed.

Designing a Full Cover: Create a full cover that includes the front, back, and spine. Ensure your cover design is professional and visually appealing. Use tools like Canva or hire a designer to create a high-quality cover.

Setting Competitive Prices: Price your paperback competitively to attract readers. Consider factors like printing costs, market trends, and your target audience's willingness to pay.

Marketing and Promotion: Promote your paperback alongside your eBook. Use social media, email newsletters, and author websites to announce the availability of your print edition. Leverage book launches and signing events to attract attention.

Expanded Distribution: If using IngramSpark, take advantage of their expanded distribution network to reach bookstores, libraries, and online retailers. This can significantly increase your book's visibility and sales.

Case Study: Expanding Reach with POD

An indie author published a memoir and wanted to offer both eBook and paperback versions. They used Amazon KDP Print to publish their paperback, benefiting from the seamless integration with their KDP account.

Mastering Amazon Publishing

To reach a broader audience, the author also used IngramSpark for expanded distribution. This allowed their book to be available in bookstores and libraries worldwide.

The author invested in professional formatting and cover design to ensure their paperback was of high quality. They set a competitive price and promoted the print edition through social media, email newsletters, and book signing events.

The combination of high-quality printing, competitive pricing, effective promotion, and expanded distribution led to increased visibility and sales. The author successfully leveraged POD to reach more readers and enhance their book's success.

Print-On-Demand services offer a cost-effective and flexible way for authors to offer physical copies of their books. By choosing the right POD service, formatting for print, designing a professional cover, setting competitive prices, and leveraging expanded distribution, you can maximize your book's reach and boost sales. POD is a valuable tool for authors looking to expand their audience and achieve long-term success in the publishing world.

9
Harnessing the Power of Customer Reviews

Encouraging and Managing Customer Reviews for Success

Customer reviews are a critical factor in the success of your book on Amazon. They influence potential readers' buying decisions and affect your book's ranking in search results. This chapter explores strategies for encouraging and managing customer reviews to build credibility and boost sales.

The Importance of Customer Reviews

Social Proof: Reviews provide social proof, helping potential readers trust your book's quality and content. Positive reviews can significantly impact purchasing decisions.

Algorithm Influence: Amazon's algorithm considers the number and quality of reviews when ranking books in search results and recommendations. More reviews can lead to higher visibility and increased sales.

Reader Feedback: Reviews offer valuable feedback from readers, helping you understand what they like and areas for improvement. This feedback can guide your future writing and marketing efforts.

Mastering Amazon Publishing

Encouraging Genuine Reviews

Ask for Reviews: Politely ask readers to leave a review if they enjoyed your book. Include a request at the end of your book, in your email newsletter, or on your social media channels.

Engage with Your Audience: Build a relationship with your readers through social media, email newsletters, and author websites. Engaged readers are more likely to leave reviews.

Use Amazon's Programs: If eligible, participate in Amazon's Vine Program, which provides free copies of your book to trusted reviewers in exchange for honest reviews.

Book Review Services: While paying for reviews is not allowed, you can use legitimate book review services that comply with Amazon's policies. These services often send review copies to potential reviewers without guaranteeing a positive review.

Advanced Review Copies (ARCs): Send ARCs to book bloggers, influencers, and reviewers before your book's release. This can help generate buzz and gather reviews early on.

Managing Reviews

Monitor Reviews: Regularly check your reviews to understand reader feedback. This can provide valuable insights into what readers like and areas for improvement.

Respond Professionally: Respond to reviews professionally and courteously, especially negative ones. Thank reviewers for their feedback and address any concerns constructively.

Report Violations: If you notice any reviews that violate Amazon's policies, report them through Amazon's review reporting system.

Case Study: Building Credibility Through Customer Reviews

An indie author published a romance novel and understood the importance of customer reviews for building credibility and boosting sales. They implemented several strategies to encourage reviews:

- **Email Newsletter**: The author built an email list of engaged readers and sent out newsletters asking for reviews.
- **Social Media Engagement**: They actively engaged with readers on social media, creating a loyal community that was eager to support their work.
- **Advanced Review Copies**: The author sent ARCs to book bloggers and reviewers, resulting in early reviews and increased visibility.

As reviews started to come in, the author monitored and responded to them professionally. They thanked reviewers for positive feedback and addressed any constructive criticism with grace. This approach helped the author build a solid reputation, leading to more sales and a growing reader base.

Customer reviews are crucial for the success of your book on Amazon. By encouraging genuine reviews, engaging with your audience, using legitimate review services, and managing reviews professionally, you can build credibility and boost your book's visibility and sales. Positive reviews can significantly impact your book's success and help you achieve your publishing goals.

Mastering Amazon Publishing

10
Amazon Author Central

Optimizing Your Author Profile and Leveraging Author Central Tools

Amazon Author Central is a valuable resource for authors, providing tools to manage your author profile, track book sales, and engage with readers. This chapter explores how to optimize your author profile and leverage Author Central tools to enhance your book's visibility and success.

Setting Up Your Author Profile

Create an Author Central Account: Sign in to Amazon Author Central using your Amazon account credentials. If you don't have an account, create one to get started.

Complete Your Author Bio: Write a compelling author bio that highlights your background, achievements, and writing journey. Include personal anecdotes and professional accomplishments to connect with readers.

Add Author Photos: Upload high-quality author photos to your profile. Include both professional headshots and casual images to give readers a sense of your personality.

Mastering Amazon Publishing

Link Your Books: Ensure all your published books are linked to your author profile. This helps readers find all your works in one place and enhances your author brand.

Include Social Media Links: Add links to your social media profiles and author website. This encourages readers to follow you and stay updated on your latest news and releases.

Leveraging Author Central Tools

Track Sales Data: Use Author Central to monitor your book's sales data and performance metrics. This information can help you make informed decisions about your marketing and promotional strategies.

Update Book Details: Keep your book details up to date, including descriptions, keywords, and categories. This ensures your book remains relevant and discoverable.

Respond to Reviews: Use Author Central to monitor and respond to customer reviews. Engaging with reviewers shows that you value their feedback and can build a positive relationship with your readers.

Add Editorial Reviews: If you have received editorial reviews or endorsements, add them to your book's detail page. These reviews can enhance your book's credibility and attract potential readers.

Customize Your Author Page: Personalize your author page with additional content, such as videos, blog posts, and event announcements. This creates a more engaging and interactive experience for your readers.

Promoting Your Author Profile

Email Signature: Include a link to your Author Central profile in your email signature. This encourages recipients to learn more about you and your books.

Social Media Promotion: Share your Author Central profile on your social media platforms. Highlight the features of your profile and invite followers to explore your books and updates.

Website Integration: Add a link to your Author Central profile on your author website. This provides a seamless way for visitors to access your profile and discover your works.

Reader Engagement: Encourage readers to visit your Author Central profile by including the link in your book's back matter, email newsletters, and promotional materials.

Case Study: Enhancing Visibility with Author Central

An indie author published a mystery series and wanted to enhance their visibility on Amazon. They set up an Author Central account and optimized their author profile with a compelling bio, high-quality photos, and links to their social media profiles.

The author regularly updated their book details, including descriptions and keywords, to ensure relevance and discoverability. They also added editorial reviews and endorsements to their book's detail pages.

To engage with readers, the author monitored and responded to customer reviews, showing appreciation for positive feedback and addressing any concerns professionally. They promoted

Mastering Amazon Publishing

their Author Central profile through email newsletters, social media, and their author website.

These efforts resulted in increased visibility, more positive reviews, and a growing reader base. Author Central proved to be a valuable tool for enhancing the author's presence on Amazon and building a loyal readership.

Amazon Author Central offers a range of tools to help authors manage their profiles, track sales, and engage with readers. By optimizing your author profile, leveraging Author Central tools, and promoting your profile, you can enhance your book's visibility and success. A well-maintained Author Central profile can help you build a strong author brand and connect with a broader audience.

About the Author

B Alan Bourgeois began his writing journey at age 12, crafting screenplays for *Adam-12* as an outlet to develop his style. While he never submitted these works, the experience fueled his passion for storytelling. After following the conventional advice of pursuing a stable career, Bourgeois rediscovered his love for writing in 1989 through a community college class, leading to his first published short story. Since then, he has written over 48 short stories, published more than 10 books, including the award-winning *Extinguishing the Light*, and made his mark in the publishing world.

Recognizing the challenges authors face, Bourgeois founded Creative House Press in the early 2000s, publishing 60 books by other authors in five years and gaining insights into the industry's marketing needs. In 2011, he launched the Texas Authors Association, which grew to include two nonprofits promoting Texas writers and literacy. He also created innovative programs like the Lone Star Festival and short story contests for students, and in 2016, the Authors Marketing Event, offering a groundbreaking Certification program for book marketing expertise.

Despite setbacks during the COVID-19 pandemic, Bourgeois adapted by launching the Authors School of Business, providing essential tools for authors to succeed as "Authorpreneurs." As publishing evolves, he has explored NFTs as a potential revenue stream for writers. With decades of experience, Bourgeois remains a driving force in the literary community, committed to helping authors thrive in a changing industry.

Bourgeois is currently the director of the Texas Authors Museum & Institute of History, based in Austin, Texas

Mastering Amazon Publishing

Other Books by the Author in this Series

Y'all Write: A Month-Long Guide to Achieving Your Writing Goals

Unlock your creative potential with *Y'all Write: A Month of Writing Celebration and Growth*! This guide offers tips, motivation, and tools to help writers of all levels set goals, build momentum, and embrace the joy of storytelling.

Author's Roadmap to Success: Proven Strategies for Thriving in Publishing

Unlock the secrets to literary success with *Author's Roadmap to Success: Proven Strategies for Thriving in Publishing*. This essential guide provides actionable strategies to help writers build strong habits, master self-publishing, and thrive in their writing careers.

B Alan Bourgeois

The Writer's Self-Care Guide: Top Ten Steps to Balance and Thrive

Transform your writing journey with *The Writer's Self-Care Guide: Top Ten Steps to Balance and Thrive*. This practical guide offers actionable steps to nurture your creativity, set boundaries, and achieve a balanced, fulfilling writing life.

Top Ten Keys for Successful Writing and Productivity

Unlock your writing potential with *Top Ten Keys for Successful Writing and Productivity*. This guide offers actionable strategies to build consistent habits, manage time effectively, and produce high-quality work to elevate your writing

Mastering Research: Top Ten Steps to Research Like a Pro

Elevate your writing with *Mastering Research: Top Ten Steps to Research Like a Pro*. This essential guide provides practical tools and techniques to conduct thorough, credible research and seamlessly integrate it into your work.

Mastering Amazon Publishing

Character Chronicles: Crafting Depth and Consistency in Creative Projects

Bring your characters to life with *Character Chronicles: Crafting Depth and Consistency in Creative Projects*. This essential guide reveals professional techniques to develop authentic, complex characters that resonate across any creative medium.

Editing Essentials: Your Guide to Finding the Perfect Editor

Transform your manuscript with *Editing Essentials: Your Guide to Finding the Perfect Editor*. This guide provides practical steps to identify, evaluate, and collaborate with the ideal editor to elevate your writing.

AI Programs Apps Authors Should Use

Revolutionize your writing with *Top Ten AI Programs Authors Should Use*. This guide explores powerful AI tools like Grammarly and Scrivener, offering practical tips to enhance creativity, productivity, and efficiency.

B Alan Bourgeois

The Business of Writing

Master the publishing world with *Unlocking the Business of Writing*. This essential guide provides expert advice and practical tips to build your author platform, maximize royalties, and turn your passion into a thriving career.

Creating an Effective Book Cover

Create a book cover that captivates readers with *Top Ten Keys to Creating an Effective Book Cover*. This guide offers expert tips and practical advice on design, branding, and marketing to make your book stand out.

Mastering the Art of the Sales Pitch

Master the art of the sales pitch with *Mastering the Art of the Sales Pitch*. This guide provides essential strategies to captivate your audience, highlight your book's value, and drive its success.

Mastering Amazon Publishing

Publishing Issues Authors Deal With

Overcome publishing challenges with *Publishing Issues Authors Deal With*. This guide offers practical strategies and expert insights to help you navigate rejection, editing, marketing, and more to achieve your publishing dreams.

The Indie Author Advantage: Mastering Control, Royalties, and Reach for Self-Publishing Success

Thrive as an indie author with *The Indie Author Advantage: Mastering Control, Royalties, and Reach for Self-Publishing Success*. This guide offers actionable strategies to retain creative control, maximize royalties, and reach a global audience.

Mastering Amazon Publishing: A Comprehensive Guide to Success for Indie Authors

Achieve self-publishing success with *Mastering Amazon Publishing: A Comprehensive Guide to Success for Indie Authors*. This guide provides proven strategies to navigate KDP, boost visibility, and maximize earnings for your books.

B Alan Bourgeois

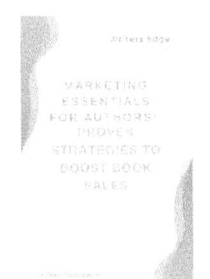

Marketing Essentials for Authors: Proven Strategies to Boost Book Sales

Boost your book sales with *Top Ten Marketing Essentials for Authors: Proven Strategies to Promote Your Book*. This guide combines traditional and digital marketing tactics to help authors effectively connect with readers and turn their books into bestsellers.

Marketing Mastery: Avoiding Common Mistakes for Authors

Master book marketing with *Marketing Mastery: Avoiding Common Mistakes for Authors*. This guide offers actionable advice to help authors connect with readers, build a strong online presence, and achieve their publishing goals.

The Author Branding Blueprint

Elevate your writing career with *Author Brand Mastery: A Comprehensive Guide to Building and Sustaining Your Unique Identity*. This guide provides practical steps to define your brand, build a professional presence, and connect meaningfully with your audience.

Mastering Amazon Publishing

Reader Magnet: Top Strategies for Building an Engaged Reader Community

Build a loyal reader community with *Reader Magnet: Top Strategies for Building an Engaged Reader Community*. This guide offers actionable strategies to connect with readers, create exclusive content, and turn your audience into passionate advocates.

Author Platform Mastery: A Comprehensive Guide to Building, Monetizing, and Growing Your Audience

Build your literary empire with *Author Platform Mastery: A Comprehensive Guide to Building, Monetizing, and Growing Your Audience*. This essential guide offers practical strategies to define your brand, engage readers, and expand your reach.

B Alan Bourgeois

Networking Success for Authors: Essential Strategies Guide

Achieve your literary goals with *Networking Success for Authors: Essential Strategies Guide*. This practical roadmap offers strategies to build meaningful connections, promote your work, and create a supportive community for lasting success.

Write, Publish, Market: The Ultimate Handbook for Author Success

ISBN:

Master the modern publishing landscape with *Write, Publish, Market: The Ultimate Handbook for Author Success*. This guide provides actionable strategies to build your author brand, attract readers, and achieve long-term success in your writing career.

Mastering Interviews: Essential Tips for Authors' Success

Excel in interviews with *Mastering Interviews: Essential Tips for Authors' Success*. This guide offers practical advice to confidently promote your work, connect with audiences, and turn every interview into a memorable success.

Mastering Amazon Publishing

Mastering Event Presentations: Avoiding Common Author Mistakes

Captivate your audience with *Mastering Event Presentations: Avoiding Common Author Mistakes*. This guide offers practical strategies to avoid pitfalls, engage your audience, and deliver impactful presentations that boost your confidence and connect with readers.

Survival Strategies for Indie Authors: Overcoming Challenges and Achieving Success

Thrive as an indie author with *Survival Strategies for Indie Authors: Overcoming Challenges and Achieving Success*. This guide provides practical advice and actionable tips to overcome obstacles, enhance your skills, and achieve your publishing goals.

Empowering Authors: Top Ten Strategies for Writing Success and Career Growth

Achieve your writing dreams with *Empowering Authors: Top Ten Strategies for Writing Success and Career Growth*. This guide offers practical advice and proven strategies to build habits, refine your craft, and grow your author career with confidence.

The Sacred Connection

Infuse your writing with mindfulness and purpose through *Creating with Spirit: The Sacred Art of Writing and Publishing*. This guide transforms your creative journey into a spiritual practice, empowering you to inspire readers and overcome challenges with authenticity and intention.

Beyond the Basics: Advanced Strategies for Indie Author Success
ISBN:

Elevate your indie publishing career with *Beyond the Basics: Advanced Strategies for Indie Author Success*. This guide offers actionable tips and strategies to diversify income, engage readers, and build a sustainable, thriving career.

The AI Author: Embracing the Future of Fiction

Embrace the future of storytelling with *The AI Author: Balancing Efficiency and Creativity in Fiction Writing*. This guide helps authors harness AI to boost productivity and creativity while preserving the emotional depth and artistry of creating.

Mastering Amazon Publishing

The Non-Fiction Nexus: Balancing AI and Human Insight in the Future of Writing

Elevate your non-fiction writing with *The Non-Fiction Nexus: Balancing AI and Human Insight in the Future of Writing.* This guide shows how to harness AI's efficiency while preserving the creativity and ethical judgment that make your work truly impactful.

Authorship Reimagined: NFTs and Blockchain Essentials

ISBN:
Embrace the future of publishing with *NFT and Blockchain Essentials for Authors' Success.* This guide explains how blockchain and NFTs can protect your work, automate royalties, and expand your audience while maximizing revenue.

Adapting Success: Your Book's Journey to Film

Turn your book into a cinematic sensation with *From Page to Screen: A Step-by-Step Guide to Adapting Your Book into a Blockbuster Film*. This guide provides practical advice and industry insights to help you navigate the adaptation process and bring your story to life on the big screen.

Beyond the Basics: Advanced Strategies for Indie Author Success

Elevate your indie publishing career with this ultimate guide to mastering advanced strategies in writing, marketing, and global distribution. Packed with actionable tips and real-world examples, it empowers authors to balance creativity with entrepreneurship and build sustainable, thriving careers.

2026: The Ultimate Year for Indie Authors

Make 2026 your breakthrough year with *The Ultimate Year for Indie Authors*. This guide offers practical strategies to optimize publishing, leverage social media, and achieve unparalleled success in your indie author journey.

Mastering Amazon Publishing